Mwy o Gynghanedd Cariad

I Eurion a Meirianwen

Investigation of New Testament Greek

How to be an Expert in saying "NO!" in Greek

God has given me the privilege of teaching my congregation at Grace Presbyterian Church, located in the Great Smoky Mountains, how to say "No!" in New Testament Greek. I have found that this Greek information is universally understood, appreciated and enjoyed by Christian people from all walks of life. Saying "No!" is a useful skill. Charles Haddon Spurgeon, the great preacher told young ministers, "If you learn how to say no to people it will be more valuable to you than learning Latin." Indeed, the Greeks realized this and developed saying "No!" into an art form. The Christian reader of the Greek New Testament, therefore, is the great beneficiary of this ancient "Just say No" campaign. But sometimes the local congregation can take it a bit too far. For instance, each year when I publicly ask the congregation for a big-fat-raise from the pulpit, I get a collective *"ou me"* (pronounced "oo may") from the people.[27] This is the strongest way in the Greek language of denying something (in this case extra cash for the pastor!). Even so, it is gratifying to know that my congregation has learned enough Greek that the words *"ou me"* flow out of their lips as clear as the Hebrew "Amen." But my congregation has gained a much greater benefit from their knowledge of *"ou me"*. As you will learn, this simple but powerful phrase (used over 90 times in the N.T) conveys powerful theology to the reader of the Bible.

The Greek people became the expert of experts on how to say "No!" in various ways and settings. This gift of saying "No!" was used by the Holy Spirit in writing His holy account of the salvation that is found in Christ. Did you know that the Pony Express Motto (now the U.S. Postal slogan) was taken from an ancient Greek piece of literature? The famous motto goes like "**Neither** snow, **nor** rain, **nor** heat, **nor** gloom of night stays these couriers from the swift completion of their appointed rounds." The Greeks were the ones who perfected this slogan that we still use today. They teach us how to produce multiple, creative ways of saying "No!" We find this slogan in Classical Greek literature in 430 B.C. Here they pile one negative upon another (four in all) to emphasize the point that is contained in this motto: nothing will stop the currier from arriving at his destination. This same determination is shown by the New Testament writers when they adopt some of these fascinating ways of communicating the word "No!" For instance, Romans 8:38-39 speaks of the amazing, unchangeable love of God. It organizes its message of never-being-separated-from-the-love-of-God-in-Christ in a memorable way by using the Greek's creative manner of saying "No!" Observe the passage as follows:

> For I am convinced that **neither (oute)** death, **nor** life, **nor** angels, **nor** principalities, **nor** things present, **nor** thing to come, **nor** powers, **nor** height, **nor** depth, **nor** any other created thing, shall be able to separate us from the love of God, which is in Christ Jesus our Lord.

In this verse, the Greek negative *oute* is used ten times to thoroughly get across the idea that at no time any believer will be separated from the love of God in Christ. Here the Apostle Paul declares our eternal security in Christ's love by employing the Greek flair of multiplying negatives. This verse, with its obvious stylish cadence, still speaks to our own generation. Consider the horrific tragedy that occurred in American on September 11, 2001. In response to this mass carnage and murder, the United States of America united in corporate prayer on the National Day of Remembrance and Mourning on September 14 in the National Cathedral in our Nation's Capital. President George W. Bush got up to speak to the Nation during this very hour. What did he say? What would you have said, if given the opportunity? President Bush quoted Romans 8:39 in his address to emphasize that, even in tragedy, nothing can separate us from the love of God.

Amazing, isn't it? In our great hour of trial we quote Romans 8:39, which just happened to be written in Greek under God's inspiration. Indeed, those who trust in God and His Promises have a great peace (Psalm 119:165).

The Greek's had three basic ways of getting the point of "No!" across to people. These three ways are on a graded scale. The Greek word *me* is a mild and conditional way of saying "No!" The word *ou* is a strong and unconditional way of saying no. Putting them together as a double negative in the phrase *ou me* was their absolutely strongest way of saying "No!" This manner was a categorical "No!" that left "No!" room for loopholes or ambiguity. It means "by no means or by any means." Here is a very famous way of explaining these distinctions:

> Dr. A.T. Robertson has the happy way of illustrating to his students the difference in meaning of these negatives by picturing graphically a young man proposing to his lady friend. If she answers him, ***me***, it may only mean that she wants to be coaxed a little longer, or that she is still in a state of uncertainty; but if she responds, ***ou***, he may as well get his hat and leave at once.[28]

So we get a sense of how the Greeks said "No!" in various circumstances.

Now let's zero in on the strongest way of saying "No!" in Greek to get a brilliant insight into this amazing language. The phrase *ou me* with the subjunctive mood, as discussed above, is the strongest way of saying "No!" in Greek. It removes all possibility; it communicates the actual reality in a crisp and clear manner. It leaves no room for uncertainty or ambiguity. This is a categorical denial of a certain, specific concept. It means to take "No!" as your final answer! If we apply this usage to A.T. Robertson's example of the young man proposing to the young woman, the young man should realize that he should never broach this question again. Her answer is final and will never change.

To review, *ou me* states a denial or a prohibition emphatically. It is rarely used in the Greek language but when used it is considered to be very emphatic. The denial it expresses is unconditional and final. With such an absolute method of communicating a negation of a specific idea, the Greeks provided the writers of the New Testament the capacity to write some amazing theological truths that assure us completely of their validity. *Ou me* is an extremely useful way to convey truth in a forthright, focused and definitive manner.

The Greek text is the final court of appeals on all matters of controversies within the church. Reformed Christian doctrine states, ". . . the New Testament in Greek (the language most widely known internationally at the time the New Testament was written) was directly inspired by God and have been kept uncontaminated throughout time by His special care and providence. They are therefore authentic and are to be the church's ultimate source of appeal in every religious controversy."[29] Consider the doctrine of Eternal Security from the perspective of the Double Negative. The doctrine of eternal security in Reformed Christian teaching may be stated as follows:

> Those whom God has accepted in His Son and has effectually called and sanctified by His Spirit <u>can never completely</u> or finally fall out of their state of grace. Rather, <u>they shall definitely continue</u> in that state to the end and <u>are eternally saved</u>.
> This endurance of the saints does not depend on their own free will but on God's unchangeable decree of election, flowing from his voluntary, unchangeable love. It also depends on the effectiveness of the merit and intercession of Jesus Christ . . . "[30] (underlines added by author)

The authors of *The Westminster Confession of Faith* here are extremely emphatic about their assertion of eternal security. Notice the absolute statements made in the underline words such as "can NEVER completely or finally fall", "they shall DEFINITELY continue in that state to the end" or "are ETERNALLY saved." The words "never, definitely and eternally" are crisp, clear words that leave no room for ambiguity on this doctrine. So how could the writers of this confession of faith write such absolute statements about eternal security when they knew that it was a controversial topic? Apparently in their minds there was NO controversy. To them there was a very clear teaching of Scripture. I suggest they knew this because of the Greek's language's capacity to say "No!" in a definitive, unconditional manner.

Consider the teaching of Jesus in John 10:28, which says "and I will give eternal life to them (*His sheep*, see verse 27), and they shall **never** perish." The word "never" is the Greek *ou me!* Remember this is a double negative of emphatic emphasis that means "never by any means" or "by no means" will this occur. Here we have a definitive statement by Jesus himself about the doctrine of eternal security for believers. Jesus' mind is made up on this issue—once He saves you, you are then saved forever! The Holy Spirit could have used just *me* to communicate this truth but that might have implied that there were exceptions to this general rule. The Spirit could have used *ou* which would have made it clear that "never" means just that "never." However, the Holy Spirit chose *ou me* which clearly showed a strong, highlighted point of precise thought—you are eternally safe in the loving arms of your Lord and Savior, Jesus. As Denver Seminary Greek professor Dr. Donald W. Burdick writes, "(a fall from grace for the true believer) is impossible in the light of Jesus' clear declaration that He gives His sheep eternal life and 'they shall never perish' (John 10:28). Here is a categorical statement of the strongest possible denial, made up of the double Greek negative, *ou me*, and the temporal phrase *eis ton aiona*, which means 'to eternity, eternally, in perpetuity', or with the negative, 'never, not at all, never again'. A person who has eternal life will most certainly never perish."[31]

In addition, Dr. Burdick gives an exceptional explanation and defense of eternal security when he writes:

> On the one hand, the Lord Himself plainly taught that the believer is absolutely eternally secure in his salvation. In John 10:28 He declared, "I give eternal life to them; and they shall never perish." This categorical denial is the translation of the Greek double negative, *ou me*, plus the idiom for the concept of eternal salvation (*eis ton aiona*). It should be rendered, "They shall by no means ever perish." This is looking at the matter from the divine side of the picture with the believer preserved in absolute security.
> On the other hand I John 2:27-28 looks at the matter from the human point of view. The believer does persevere. He keeps on following the good Shepherd (John 10:27). He is responsible for maintaining His relationship to Christ as the Holy Spirit teaches (I John 2:24). God guarantees the believer's security, but the Christian's regenerated will persists in maintaining a saving relationship with the Lord.[32]

This line of theological reasoning is often countered with the observation that some people who do join the church still fall away. However, I John 2:19 clearly speaks to this situation when it says, "If they had been of us, they would have remained with us." As Dr. Burdick states, "Those who are genuine members of the Christian circle will continue in the circle. Defection is the evidence that one's profession was not genuine . . . When one leaves the circle of God's people altogether, it is an indication that he never did belong to the family of God."[33]

Therefore, these words from theologian John Calvin concerning John 10:28 ring true, "It is the incomparable fruit of faith that Christ invites us to be sure and untroubled when we are brought by faith into his fold. But we must also see what basis this assurance rests on. It is that Christ will be the faithful guardian of our salvation . . . This is a remarkable passage, teaching us that the salvation of all the elect is as certain as God's power is invincible."[34] We can trust God at His word in Holy Scripture on this crucial issue. Remember that God is light and as I John 4:8 reads "and in Him there is **no** darkness at all." Here the Greek negative expresses to us an altogether awesome truth about our Heavenly Father. Dr. Burdick informs:

> The denial is made more doubly strong by the word *ouk*, "not", and *oudemia*, "no." First, the two words make up a kind of double negative, which in Greek serves to strengthen the denial. In addition, the term *oudemia* is in itself a forceful denial made up of the negative *ou* and the cardinal numeral *mia*. Literally it means *not one*. Thus there is not one bit of darkness in God, not the slightest trace of moral evil. He is absolutely holy and true.[35]

Once again we see incredible truth from the New Testament Greek's use of the negative. So I ask the Christian reader, "Is there any reason now to doubt God's word that you, as a true believer in our Lord Jesus Christ, will **never perish** but have eternal life?" Of course, your answer should be a robust, *ou me* in light of the New Testament Greek. Enough said!

But More to Be Noticed

Also, impressively when Jesus talks about the permanency of the Law (Old Testament) he says that "nothing *(ou me)* will ever pass away from the Law until all things are fulfilled (5:18)." In fact, as we check out a Greek New Testament concordance, we discover that Jesus liked to use the *ou me* to communicate absolute truth. One of the most dramatic places where Jesus uses the *ou me* is in Matthew 24:35, which says, "Heaven and earth shall pass away, but My words shall never *(ou me)* pass away." Therefore, we learn from the Greek negatives that we can hold confidently to the inerrant inspiration of the Old Testament (Matthew 5:18) and the New Testament (Matthew 26:24:35).

==

Putting It All Together:

Do you see how Chapters 2 and 3 go together? In Chapter 2 we learned that God may have chose Greek to write about His Son because it is an emphatic, educated, evangelical and exquisite language. In Chapter 3 we looked at the impacting nature of the Greek negative. Here we saw how definitively (vivid and emphatic) the Greek's could say "No!" and how this knowledge affects our view of the eternal security of the believer. We saw that the Greeks love of saying "No!" dates back prior to 300 B.C. so indeed it is a mature (educated) vocabulary. Additionally, we saw how eloquent the language could be (exquisite) as we reviewed the classic statement on God's love in Romans 8. Most importantly, however, the Greek language was and is used by the Holy Spirit to bring people to Jesus Christ the Shepherd and Savior of their souls (evangelical). Check out these words spoken by Jesus (John 11:25-26):

> I am the resurrection and the life; he who believes in Me shall live even if he dies, and everyone who lives and believes in Me shall never *(ou me)* die. Do you believe this?

Well, do *you*? The ***ou me*** (remember pronounced: "oo may") clearly declares that life eternal is ours if we believe in the Eternal Savior who died on the cross for our sins and was resurrected on the third day according to the Scriptures. The Good News is that everyone who calls upon the Lord Jesus will be saved forever (Romans 10:13).

Remember Erasmus saying that the Greek New Testament will give you insight into the blessed mind of Jesus. Hearing Jesus use the double negative in Greek to express His assertion that those who believe in Him will never, *ever* perish demonstrates to you the decisiveness, authority, confidence and overwhelming compassion of His mind, doesn't it? The simple question "Do you believe this?" is gently put to Martha with the grand background of Jesus being the Resurrection and the Life. Don't you spiritually sense the risen, exalted Savior Jesus asking this same question of you? Erasmus was right, wasn't he? The Greek New Testament really gives you Jesus "in an intimacy so close that He would be less visible to you if he stood before your eyes." Let's illustrate this truth with an example from an extremely reputable Greek scholar's exegesis of Mark 5:41. In this passage Jesus is seen "touching the hand of the little girl" He is going to resurrect from the dead. Dr. Wallace informs us that the phrase "touching the hand" is written with a finesse not to be missed. This Greek phrase pictures a gentle, tender touch by Jesus.[36] For sure, Jesus is the Most Powerful One (who is the resurrection) but He is also the Most Gentle One (He gives life). The Greek word pictures show us Jesus in a way that increases our understanding of Him and confirms our experience of His sovereign, loving graciousness. Isn't it an amazing thought that when the Almighty God in Christ *touched* your life with His love, He did so with this same tenderness? Someday Christ, with this same powerful yet tender touch, will resurrect all those who believe.

The H.O.P.E. Bible Study Method with the O.P.E.N. Journal

The **H.O.P.E. Bible Study Method** is an organized way to help the reader who knows little Greek get the most out of his or her New Testament. It is designed to introduce you to the impacting nature of Greek from day one of your study. Here is the outline of the **H.O.P.E. Bible Study**:

H = Holy Spirit Prayer for Illumination

O = Original New Testament Language of Greek

P = Parallel Bible Translations Consulted

E = Exegetical Note Taking

This method provides a comprehensive approach for digging into the treasures that are contained in the Greek New Testament, even for the person who has no academic training in this wonderful language.

It is critical for the Gospel reader of the Greek text to adhere to a system of Biblical study that helps him or her rightly interpret the Word of God. Nevertheless, Bible study should always have a devotional element that strengthens us in the grace of God. Romans 15:5 brilliantly reminds us, "For whatever was written in earlier times was written for our instruction, that through perseverance and the encouragement of the Scriptures we might have hope." Here is where the H.O.P.E. Bible Study System enters in. It is designed to make sure that we do **exegesis** not **eisegesis**. These two are important Greek terms that make a vital distinction for accurate Bible study and devotion. **Eisegesis** is a Greek word that means to read something *into* a text. We all have met someone who could quote a verse out of its context to suit their own personal agenda. They forget the principle that "A text without a context is only a pretext" and then act, not as a faithful interpreter, but as a ventriloquist who project their ideas on what the Biblical author meant.[37] Dedicated Christians are not interested in hearing their own voices or someone else's opinion about the text. What our hearts are eager to hear is the voice of God from the pages of the Holy Bible. Therefore, the Greek word **exegesis** is a guardian of the message of God for it literally means to read *out of* the text.[38] This means that the context around the verse is the supreme and authoritative interpreter of the Biblical text that we are studying. Only then will we hear the authentic voice of the Holy Spirit and be inspired with hope from the one who originally inspired the Scriptures (2 Peter 1:20-21). Eugene Peterson's words are apt here:

> . . . exegesis is an act of love. It means loving the one who speaks the words enough to want to get the words right. It is respecting the words enough to use every means we have to get the words right. Exegesis is loving God enough to stop and listen carefully. It follows that we bring leisure and attentiveness of lovers to this text, cherishing every comma and semicolon, relishing the oddness of this preposition, delighting in the surprising placement of this noun . . . it (the Bible) is given to us as a text intended to form a whole life to the glory of God.[39]

Therefore, I believe the safest three rules in properly interpreting the Bible are these:

- Always let Scripture interpret Scripture. In this endeavor make sure you allow the clearer Scriptures to help you interpret the more puzzling ones (2 Peter 3:14-16).[40]

- Make sure you remain humble before God and His Word (1 Peter 5:6). A good part of being humble is adhering to a system of "checks and balances." Of course, the most important check and balance is the above principle of letting Scripture interpret Scripture. But also it is good to ask for the wisdom of other Bible interpreters to make sure that you are on solid ground in your understanding of Scripture. Check it out in a creditable, evangelical commentary or from a Bible believing pastor.

- Remember language has a tendency to surprise you.[41] For instance, all words have a range of meanings.[42] Also, these meanings are anchored to a particular historical period. Plus, the writer may be actually coining a new meaning or use of a traditional word. All of these factors and more keep the Bible student in a teachable state. This teachable spirit should also translate into defending the essential, historic truths of the Christian faith Jude 3). Nothing in the Greek text, rightly understood, undermines one doctrine in the Apostles' Creed or the Nicene Creed. In fact, as you will see in this workbook, the Greek New Testament clearly teaches these great truths.

Holy Spirit Illumination

Nothing is more important than this first part. Before any Christian reads the Bible he or she should ask the Holy Spirit of God for understanding. After all, the Holy Spirit, the third Person of the Holy Trinity, is the Author of the Bible. So it is imperative that we show respect and reverence for the Author of the Bible. He, in fact, indwells the Christian and will teach him the truth of salvation. Theologian R.C. Sproul explains it this way:

> Though the Scriptures themselves are light for us, there is need for additional illumination so that we may clearly perceive the light. The same Holy Spirit who inspires the Scripture, works to illumine the Scriptures for our benefit. He sheds more light on the original light. Illumination is the work of the Holy Spirit. He helps us to hear, receive, and properly understand the message of God's Word (1 Corinthians 2:9-11).
> The Spirit is still working to illumine what is revealed in Scripture. The Spirit helps us to understand the Bible, convict us of

> the truth of the Bible, and to apply that truth to our lives. He works with the Word and through the Word. His task is never to teach against the Word. It is therefore always necessary to test what we hear by the teaching of the Scripture. The Scripture is the Spirit's book.[43]

Therefore, we see the critical importance of relying upon the Holy Spirit's assistance and illumination in properly understanding the Scripture (John 16:13-15 & 2Peter 1:21).

How do we seek the Holy Spirit's help in reading the Bible? We pray to the Lord, asking Him to grant us this Divine Teacher's insights into our study of the Holy Bible. Always pray to God asking Him for illumination before you seek God's truth in the Scriptures.[44] God receives glory in our asking Him for illumination. Here are some great Prayers of Illumination from Psalm 119:[45]

> Open my eyes, that I may behold
>
> Wonderful things from Thy law. (18)
>
> The earth is full of Thy loving-kindness,
>
> > O Lord,
>
> Teach me Thy statues. (64)
>
> Thou are good and doest good;
>
> > Teach me Thy statues. (68)
>
> Thy hands made me and fashioned me;
>
> Give me understanding, that I may learn
>
> Thy commandments. (73)

All in all, as you pray these prayers of illumination, you'll discover the truth of, "Thy word is a lamp to my feet, And a light to my path (105)."

Original Greek Language

As a first step in your study, I recommend that you secure a good, solid Greek-English Interlinear New Testament. [46] This type of New Testament will parallel the Greek and the English words.[47] In other words you'll see the Greek text and the English text side by side. This will result in a better understanding of the New Testament even if you don't know a letter of Greek. By seeing the Greek and English side by side you'll be able to at least see the Greek word order of the sentence that you are studying. Seeing the order of the sentence in the Greek language can produce wonderful insights. My favorite example is the famous passage in Hebrew 13:8 which reads, "Jesus Christ is the same yesterday and today, yes and forever." Now let's look at it like an Interlinear would:

Iesous Christos echthes kai semeron o autos   kai eis tous aionas

Jesus   Christ yesterday and today   **the same** and unto the ages.

You quickly spot that that phrase "the same" is seemingly out of place as compared to the smooth English translation. But there is something wonderful about where the Greek places this phrase "the same," isn't there? By placing it in this position of the sentence it actually underscores the truth that our Lord and Savior NEVER CHANGES and that He is THE SAME for the Christian in the book of Hebrews as well as the Christians living in the 21st Century. Christ's impeccable faithfulness is to be praised and adored forever in all generations—including our own personal lives!

As you consistently begin to consult the Greek text of the New Testament Interlinear you will become more and more familiar with the Greek words of the Bible. This is exciting and gives inspiration in trying to pursue further Greek word studies. For the layman, this knowledge also helps you to better check out what the Bible teachers and preachers are teaching like those in Berea did (Acts 17:10-12). Finally, if you like art or calligraphy (Greek for "beautiful writing") you'll love some of the sights in the Greek New Testament. Take Hebrews 13:8 for example. This verse could be arranged as follows:

Iesous Christos	=	"Jesus Christ
echthes	=	yesterday
kai	=	and
semeron	=	today
o autos	=	the same
kai	=	and
eis tous aionas	=	forever."

This is masterfully arranged to show us some of the grand beauty of the Greek behind this well-known verse. Dr. Lane observes, "The unusual word order is calculated to arouse and focus the attention . . . 'Jesus Christ' is emphatic by virtue of its position at the beginning of the sentence."[48] Here the Greek word order brings glory to our wonderful Savior.

Parallel Bible Translations

One of the most efficient ways to study the Bible is to consult a number of parallel translations. Standard versions are the King James (KJV), New American Standard (NASB) and the New International (NIV). The Gospel of Jesus Christ comes clearly through in each of these translations of the original Greek text. Each translation has its advantages and disadvantages.[49] However, taken together, they can really help the Bible student understand some of the nuances that are contained in the Greek text. The

NASB is closet to the Greek text of the New Testament so it should always be consulted. The KJV obviously helps us see how our forefathers would have translated a particular text so this is valuable information from our sacred history. The NIV shows us how to use modern words to faithfully translate a Biblical text. Consulted together, these three versions will give your Bible devotions a balanced and enhanced view of the Greek behind the English translations.[50]

Exegetical Bible Note Taking

The key to solid Bible study is to take plenty of notes. When you see something in the Scriptures that strikes you as significant you should get into the practice of writing it down. This practice does a number of helpful things. First, it assists you in better memorizing the Scriptures and what they teach. Second, you may develop follow up questions from these notes to ask your pastor or to research further as you consult the commentaries. As you speak about your findings with other knowledgeable Christians (such as your pastor) and read quality biblical commentaries they will act as a check and balance to your private Bible study. Third, it is a discipline that will make you into a more precise student of the Word. By paying such focused attention to the context of the verse, it will help guard your thinking by way of exegesis and not eisegesis. In reference to note taking and the Greek text, I suggest you practice the **O.P.E.N. Journal**:

O = Organization: How is the Bible text arranged?

P = Pictures: Are their any Gospel word pictures within the Bible text?

E = Emphatics: What does the Greek text assert as true or as false?

N = Nexus words: What connections does the writer want the reader to make?

These questions are the heart of this Bible study method of using a New Testament English-Greek Interlinear and an introductory knowledge of the Greek language. Through these questions, your eyes will be opened to some of the wonderful things in God's Holy Word.[51]

For instance, you've already seen in Hebrews 13:8 that the word order (Organization) of the Greek text might enhance your understanding of the Biblical verse. This study approach alone will revolutionize your Bible study. If you would like to extend your study of Scripture in this way, please contact me at this E-mail address: impactgreek@hotmail.com for further materials that can be ordered to assist you in this illuminating journey through the Greek gems of the New Testament. Now let's look at a few examples of how this approach to Bible study works:

Bible Devotion on Titus 1:2

Let's say your morning devotion today will be on Titus 1:2 and you are committed to following the H.O.P.E. Bible Study System. What would this look like? First you honor the Author of the Bible, the Holy Spirit, and ask Him to bring illumination to your heart as to what He desires to teach you this morning from the New Testament (Holy Spirit Prayer of Illumination). Second, as you read Titus 1:2 you particularly notice the part that says that God doesn't lie to you or anyone. In your New Testament Interlinear (Original Greek Language), you begin to get a feel for the Greek word order in doing this step and seeing how the interlinear translator handled the text. In this case Dr. Alfred Marshall writes:

    Greek: o apseudes Theos

    English: the   unlying   God

Third, you'd consult at least three translations and compare and contrast them as follows:

NASB " . . .which God, who cannot lie . . ."

KJV " . . . which God, that cannot lie . . . "

NIV " . . . which God, who does not lie . . . "

Fourth, you now begin to make Exegetical Notes in your OPEN Journal. You see plainly that this text is asserting something about God. The Greeks are famous for using the Greek letter alpha (a) before a word to negate it (such as the Greek word **a**pseudes in Titus 1:2 which means non-lying). We see this often in English. For instance, the word atheist is broken down as follows: *a* means "non" and *theist* means a "believer in God" so, putting it together, an atheist is a non-believer in God or doesn't-believe-in-God is this person's particular belief. The alpha privative before the word negates that term. Here in Titus 1:2 we see literally "**the non-lying God.**" Therefore, we can trust all the promises He makes to His children because He does not and cannot lie. This is essential to His holy nature. This assertion about God is significant because it truly does gives us a basis for our hope of eternal life—the holy, truthful character of God Himself. Even so, we wish to consult other knowledgeable people about the Bible and Greek to see what they say about this text. We read Dr. Heibert's comments:

> The remainder of verse two and the first part of verse three describe this eternal life. It is grounded in God's past promise and has been manifested in the Gospel.
> This life was the subject of divine promise, 'Which (life) God, who cannot lie, promised before times eternal." The hope is sure because the realization of the promise rests upon the character of God. He is the God "who cannot lie" (literally, "the-un-lie-able God"). He is the absolutely faithful and true God; His promise is sure of fulfillment.[52]

Now, contrast the Greek "the-un-lie-able God" with the English version. What's the difference? Of course, the word order is different. Personally, the N.T. Greek's "the-un-lie-able God" sounds like a title for God (the article **o** in front of it would support this), which gives even more stress to the faithfulness and truthfulness of God.

Bible Devotion on Hebrews 13:5b

Let's say you are home from a tiring, bothersome day at work and you desire to do your evening devotions on Hebrews 13:5b. You've got a little more time than in the early morning hours so you really want to dig into the text. First, you spend considerable time in a Prayer of Illumination to the Holy Spirit asking Him guide you. You're relying on the Holy Spirit for insight and inspiration to impact your relationship with Jesus Christ the Lord. Second, you consult the original Greek by using an Interlinear. Here is what you see:

ou me   se   ano

By no (any) means   you   will I leave

oud'

nor

ou me   se   egkatalipo

By no (any) means   you   I forsake

Based on your knowledge of how to say "No!" in Greek from chapter three, you notice that ***ou me*** is used twice in this Bible verse. You become extremely excited because you know that double negative is rare and such a find must contain deep truths for the Bible reader. That deep truth, of course, is that God is always there for you!

Third, you consult at least three translations of Hebrews 13:5. Here is what you discover:

NASB: Let your character be free from the love of money, being content with what you have; for He Himself has said, "I WILL NEVER DESERT YOU, NOR WILL I EVER FORSAKE YOU."

KJV: Let your conversation be without covetousness; and be content with such things as ye have: for he hath said, I will never leave thee, nor forsake thee.

NIV: Keep your lives free from the love of money and be content with what you have, because God has said, "Never will I leave you; never will I forsake you."

Now you're ready to begin to take some Exegetical notes in your O.P.E.N Journal.

You look at the arrangement and organization of the words in Greek. What do you see? You've already noticed that the final two clauses begin with the *ou me*. The doctrine of the eternal-faithful presence of God clearly, emphatically comes through, doesn't it? The double use of the *ou me* in this portion of the revealed Word of God establishes this beyond any reasonable doubt. You can certainly write in your O.P.E.N. Journal assertions about God and what His will is for your life. On one hand, Hebrews 13:5b is a breathtaking view of the glory of the never failing, never-ending presence of God towards feeble sinners like you and me! On the other hand, it breathes new life into us for it is God's personal Word to us. This result is no less real than when God breathed life into Adam at the time of creation (Genesis 2:7).

The Bible is God breathed according to 2 Timothy 3:16. Dr. Ryrie writes, "The entire Bible is God-*breathed* . . . The form is passive, meaning that the Bible is the result of the breath of God . . . Our English word *inspire* carries the idea of breathing into something. But here we are told that God breathed *out* something, namely, the Scripture."[53] We are imbued with the very breath of God in His Holy Word.[54] The Rabbi's used to contend, "If a man loses a coin in his house he kindles many lights, and seeks till he finds it. If for something which affords only an hour's life in this world, a man kindles many lights, and searches till he find it, how much more should you dig as for hidden treasure after the words of the Law, which gives life both in this world and in the world-to-come" (*Song of Songs Rabbah* 1:9)

Let's get to the discovery . . . but wait (!) . . . the light is still shining from Hebrews 13:5. As we observe God's Word, the Holy Spirit trains us to dig up the precious treasures contained therein. Here are two more points well worth knowing from this excellent verse:

- Don't just notice the Double Play **ou me** but look at the Triple Play **ou** contained within the verse. It reads never (**ou** me) will I leave thee nor (**ou**de—a strong way of saying "No!" as well) and never (**ou** me) will I forsake you. It doesn't get anymore unambiguous than this—God is the Immanuel (which means "God with us," see Matthew 1:23) and He will never stop being that for you!
- Notice the word **autos**. This is an emphatic term in the Greek text. It means God Himself (autos) has promised His ever-supporting presence to you.

It reveals that the Holy Spirit is a Divine Artist who speaks with a sophisticated, fine-tuned flair. Indeed, the Greek writing style here is a masterpiece of glory and grace. Hopefully, you will now be able to testify to family and friends that *you've seen* how the Greek New Testament speaks powerfully, precisely and in a most precious way.[55]

===

Putting it all together . . .

Remember in Chapter 3 you learned about the Greek Double Negative. Here in Chapter 4 you were able to apply that new knowledge to Hebrews 13:5. But more importantly, you see how Hebrews 13:5 confirms the observation made in Chapter 2 that the Greek was chosen by God because it was emphatic, educated, evangelical and exquisite. Hebrew 13:5 is emphatic (the Double Play *ou me* and Triple Play *ou* prove that). Hebrews 13:5 is educated (there is an obvious flair crafted from the classical Greek). It is evangelical (There is no greater message to the human heart than the fact that God Himself (autos) has communicated His eternal love for you!). Mostly it is definitely exquisite for it both takes your breath away and breathes new life into you at the very same time. Now, let me add one more reason why God may have chose Greek to communicate the Gospel of His Son. It is a language that handles **emotions** well. Think about this: God who so loved the world (John 3:16) and who so loved his Son (Matthew 3:17) would certainly want to powerfully, yet tenderly speak to us about what's in His heart, right? In fact, the Greek New Testament as it was inspired by the Holy Spirit (Romans 5:5, 8) does this marvelously well. As Kenneth S. Wuest observed, "Every word (of the Greek N.T.) is alive with divine life because it was chosen by the Holy Spirit and energized with divine fire from the altars of heaven itself."

Insights into New Testament Greek

Calligraphy Greek

Our word calligraphy comes from a Greek word that means beautiful writing. The Greek New Testament contains numerous beautifully-crafted written doctrinal declarations. Many of the Bible translations of the Greek New Testament do their best to give a glimpse into its majestic and sonorous style. Nevertheless, there is nothing like gazing on the original masterpiece it its full glory. Here are four examples from the Greek New Testament designed to give a glimpse into the glory of the Holy Spirit's writing style.

1. Our Peace in Christ

Jesus says in the literal word order of John 16:33 that "these things I have spoken to you that in me peace you may have." In English this teaching that we have peace in Christ is absolutely wonderful but the Greek text adds a brilliant and special artistic touch. Let's look at this from an interlinear perspective:

en emoi eirenen echete

in me   peace   you may have

The Greek-English interlinear shows the self-evident alliteration that every word in the phrase from Jesus begins with the Greek letter Epsilon (e). This is not only artistic but helps the disciples in memorizing this encouraging slogan from Jesus our Lord. Also, the four eloquent Epsilons in succession demonstrate artistically the close integration of Jesus, the Christian and peace. Marvelous truth is revealed simply by observing the miniature letters of the Greek New Testament.

2. Our Praise to God

The hymn "Immortal, Invisible" by Walter Chalmers Smith is based on 1 Timothy 1:17. The words immortal, invisible are excellent recreations of the alliteration found in the original Greek text. The adjectives *immortal, invisible* both start with the letter "I", when sung in succession, produce a catchy and sonorous cadence. Again, let's look at this verse from the perspective of the Greek-English interlinear:

to   de   basilei   ton   **a**ionon,   **a**phtharto,   **a**orato . . .

to the   now   King   of the   ages   incorruptible   invisible

The interlinear clearly shows forth the triple-play Alpha (a) alliteration in the three adjectives describing God. Dr. J. Ramsey Michaels observes, "The three adjectives with the negating prefix **a-** represents a classic negative way of characterizing persons or things that strain one's descriptive powers." [56]

In a stunning literary *inclusio* 1 Timothy 1:17 *starts* with a triple-play Alpha alliteration and *finishes* with one as well marking this God-centered doxology with dignified bookends. The doxology concludes "unto the ages (**a**ionas) of the ages (**a**ionon). Amen (**a**men)."

3. Precious Blood of God's Son

The Apostle Peter, under the inspiration of the Spirit of the Living God, writes these sacred words in 1 Peter 1:18-19 . . .

> For you know that it was not with perishable things such as
>
> silver or gold that you were redeemed from the empty way
>
> of life handed down to you from your forefathers,

> but (**a**lla) with the precious blood (**a**imati) of Christ,
>
> a lamb (**a**mvou) without blemish (**a**mom**ou**) or defect (**a**spil**ou**).

The focus is on the last two adjectives describing the precious blood of Jesus Christ our Lord and Savior. As Dr. Michaels says, "The paired negative adjectives gain a rhetorical effect by their similar endings and their repeated **a-** prefix . . . "[57] In an attempt to recreate the precious sounds that the identical endings of these two words would have produced for a Greek listener, Michaels translates it as follows, "but with the precious blood, like that of a **f**ault**less** and **f**law**less** lamb—the blood of Christ . . . " As the early church wrote, "Let us fix our attention on the *blood* of Christ *and realize that it is precious to his Father* . . ." (emphasis added) The beautiful alliteration and the dignified cadence of the Greek text of 1 Peter 1:19 gives evidence of how much the Heavenly Father loves His only begotten Son and how infinite is His endorsement of the work of Christ upon the cross.

4. Our Promised Inheritance

According to 1 Peter 1:4, we have "an indestructible (in Greek starts with an Alpha—verify this by looking this verse up in a Greek-English Interlinear New Testament), incorruptible (in Greek starts with an Alpha), and unfading (starts with an Alpha) inheritance." All of this is true—but notice how brilliantly it is written. Each word begins with the prefixed **a.** In this passage, because of the manner in which it is written, the diamond of our heavenly inheritance is set in a beautiful Alpha arrangement (called "alliteration").

The Autographs of God

My aim in writing this brief introduction to the spiritual impact of the Greek language was to give interested people, who have not be able to study Greek, a glimpse into the savvy, sophisticated and sterling use of Greek by the Holy Spirit in His inspired work—the New Testament. I hope you, the reader of *Impact Greek*, have sensed the joy and power of the Greek New Testament without the effort of having to take a full seminary style course in this Biblical language. It is my conviction that if every Christian student of the Bible were to get a gist of the Greek behind the New Testament translations then their spiritual knowledge and personal ethics would be positively impacted for the glory of God.

In this light, I introduce you to what I call the "autographs" of God in the New Testament. These "autographs" has brought immeasurable joy and power to Christians throughout many generations. The Greek personal pronoun *autos* (English speakers get the words "automobile" and "autopilot" from this word) in the nominative case often serve as sacred and eloquent signature of the Holy God Almighty. Let me illustrate by referring your attention to 1 Peter 5:10, which reads:

> And the God of all grace, who called you to his eternal
> glory in Christ, after you have suffered a little while,
> will himself *(autos)* restore you and make you strong,
> firm, and steadfast.

Howard Marshall writes, "Here Peter reinforces the subject of the sentence by adding the pronoun *autos*, and the force of the addition is to indicate that God is personally involved in caring for his people."[58] Peter, by using the *autos*, is emphatically stating that God is personally going to care for you—it will not be a fellow believer nor a pastor or even an angel—but the Lord himself will attend to His children. Autos (or auto) is an intense personal pronoun that God uses to sign His promises so that His people will emphatically know that the Almighty is always on their side. It is as though God's promises are like checks that He has signed and given to us so that we might deposit them in our hearts.

More "Autographs" from God

- The Promise from **God the Father** to all Christians: "Now may the God of peace Himself *(autos)* sanctify you entirely . . . (1 Thessalonians 5:23).

- The Price paid by **God the Son** for our redemption: "He himself *(autos)* bore our sins in his body on the tree . . . (1 Peter 2:24).

- The Personal ministry of **God the Holy Spirit** to the children of God: "but the Spirit Himself *(auto)* intercedes for us . . . (Romans 8:26).

Indeed, it is true that "He *(autos)* is preeminent in all things (Colossians 1:18)."

Theological Greek

The vocabulary of the Greek New Testament is worth learning because its words contain deep theological truth and its words are the foundation for so many English words. Also, it will help you in your doctrinal studies of the Bible because Christian theologians have divided theological matters using various distinctive Greek words of the New Testament. As you study your Greek-English Interlinear and begin to take notes on what you've learn, you'll discover that these Greek theological categories will help you sort out what you are learning. Knowing these theological categories will help you in two ways: a) it will focus your mind on what the passage is actually teaching about, and b) it will help you organize your theological findings. Each of these theological terms ends with the *–ology* ending. In the context of these categories it means "the study of" or "to speak about" some particular theological discipline. So, for instance, the word theology means "study of God" and those things associated with the Divine. Here is the list of these theological categories of Christian theology:

1. **Bibliology** = Study of the Bible (Biblos used 10x in the New Testament)

    *First word in the New Testament is Biblos (Matthew 1:1).

2. **Theology Proper** = Study of God the Triune One (Theos used 1317 times)

3. **Christology** = Study of Christ (Christos used 529x)

4. **Pneumatology** = Study of the Spirit (Pneuma used 379x)

5. **Anthropology** = Study of Mankind (Anthropos used 550x)

6. **Hamartiology** = Study of Sin (Harmartia used 173x)

7. **Soteriology** = Study of Salvation (Soteria used 45x)

8. **Angelology** = Study of Good and Fallen Angels (Angelos used 175x)

9. **Ecclesiology** = Study of the Church (Ecclesia used 114x)

10. **Eschatology** = Study of the Last Things (Eschatos used 52 times)

[1] In order to learn Greek you must have a working knowledge of the 24 letters in the Greek alphabet. I have not included an extensive section in this book on the Greek alphabet because there are so many competent resources that will effectively teach you the Greek alphabet. I recommend www.teknia.com to get you started in this basic but vital area of Greek knowledge. It will also teach you the principles of syllabication.

[2] Isaac Watts in his book, *The Improvement of the Mind* (p.221-222), writes these wise words: "But those that design the sacred profession of theology should make it their labour of chief importance to be very conversant with their Bibles, both in the Old and New Testament; and this requires some knowledge of those original languages, Greek and Hebrew, in which the Scriptures were written. All that will pursue these studies with honour should be able to read the Old Testament tolerably in the Hebrew tongue: at least they should be so far acquainted with it as to find out the sense of the text by the help of a dictionary. *But scarce any man should be thought worthy of the name of a solid divine, or a skillful preacher of the gospel, in these days of light and liberty, unless he has pretty good knowledge of the Greek, since all the important points of the Christian religion are derived from the New Testament, which was written in that language.*" (Emphasis added)

[3] W. Brandt and H. Lehman, ed., *Luther's Works* (Philadelphia Muhlenberg Press, 1962), pp. 357-366.

[4] John Piper, *Brothers, Bitzer Was a Banker* (The Standard, June 1983), pp. 18-19.

[5] Walter C. Kaiser, Jr., *Toward An Exegetical Theology* (Grand Rapids, Michigan: Baker Book House, 1981), p. 27.

[6] A.T. Robertson, *A Grammar Of The Greek New Testament In The Light Of Historical Research* (Nashville, Tennessee: Broadman Press, 1934), p. 565.

[7] Internet Interview of Eugene Peterson by Steve Huyser-Honig, *Eugene Peterson on God's Standing Invitation: Eat This Book* (Calvin Institute of Christian Worship, 2007).

[8] A. T. Robertson, *The Minister and His Greek New Testament* (Grand Rapids, Michigan: Baker Book House, 1977), p. 79.

[9] Gary D. Pratico and Miles V. Van Pelt, *Basics of Biblical Hebrew* (Grand Rapids, Michigan: Zondervan, 2001), pp. 135-136.

[10] H.H. Rowley, *Recent Foreign Theology* (Expository Times, 1963), p. 383.

[11] Kenneth S. Wuest, *The Practical Use of the Greek New Testament* (Chicago, Illinois: Mood Press,1946), p. 111.

[12] Ibid, p.153.

[13] There are 5,400 Greek words in the New Testament. There are over 90,000 words in the Greek language. The average 10 year old child knows about 5,000 words in his or her native language (see David Alan Black's *Lingusitics for Students of New Testament Greek*, p. 71-71). These facts resonate with my heart that God was certainly concerned about everyone who could read to be able to read His priceless Book about His precious Son. Also, learning Greek vocabulary is something that is doable for the average student and reader. I'm a living example of this fact—like Dr. Machen said, any pastor (or any Christian for that matter) of *average* intelligence can learn Greek.

[14] *Westminster Confession of Faith:* By this faith, a Christian believes to be true whatsoever is revealed in the Word, for the authority of God Himself speaking therein; and acts differently upon that which each particular passage thereof contains; yielding obedience to the commands, trembling at the threatenings, and embracing the promises of

God for this life, and that which is to come. But the principal acts of saving faith are accepting, receiving, and resting upon Christ alone for justification, sanctification, and eternal life, by virtue of the covenant of grace.

[15] *Here's one example from my devotional life:* I was reading in Ephesians the various words for God's *will*. I was getting fairly exhausted because there are quite a number of them and keeping track of their nuances was a difficult (more like impossible) juggle for my finite mind. But there it was the Holy Trinity word for the *will* of God. In English it is usually rendered God's "counsel." Of course, this begs the question who could give God counsel anyway? The obvious answer is the Holy Trinity Who knows, experiences and originated the idea of the totally loving relationship. There is only one God; even so, there are three Persons in God: The Father, the Son and the Holy Spirit who are all equal in essence, power and glory. So the Greek word for counsel is *boule*, which is pronounced *bou-lay*. This to me sounds like a name for a fine wine like the French word *Chardonnay*. This definition* for this word as applied to the Trinity and its exquisite sounding ring simply coalesced into a profound sense of joy that I was rummaging around in the cellar of the finest wines of the universe. I also worried, "What right did I have to be there listening in on the holiest of conversations within the Godhead?" Then it came to me—it was God Himself who had poured this finest of wines for me; it was God who had invited me into his cellar to sit with Him, and then suddenly I was with God who was my heavenly Host—as *the* Friend he was sharing with me the wonders of my salvation planned before time began. It was God who took the time to be with me, who shared a wine so fine that it could never be forgotten. I came away with an impression of the distinguished class and gracious hospitality of our majestic God. So now, when I wish to sip the finest wines known anywhere with the Savior of the World, I simply turn to my Greek New Testament concordance to locate *boule* this choicest of theological wines. Wine drinkers have a saying, *In Vino Veritas*, which is Latin for "in wine there is truth." After my sanctified encounter with God's wines in the New Testament Greek, you'll have no arguments from me about that motto. * Walter Bauer, William F. Arndt and F. Wilbur Gingrich, *A Greek-English Lexicon Of The New Testament and Other Early Christian Literature* (Chicago, Illinois: The University of Chicago Press, 1979, Second Edition) p. 145.

[16] John R. W. Stott, *The Gospel and the End of Time* (Downers Grove, Illinois: InterVarsity Press, 1991), p. 131.

[17] Although there are contemporary signs of people making the connection that Greek is helpful for education. For instance, some advocate knowledge of Greek will help a college applicant perform better on the SAT and the Orton-Gillingham approach to teaching reading skills to students with dyslexia (Greek for "trouble with words") introduce them to the various Greek word patterns that are consistently found in English. Also, some High School Latin teachers are integrating instruction in the Greek language within their courses.

[18] David Alan Black, *It's Still Greek To Me* (Grand Rapids, Michigan: Baker Books, 1998), p. 153.

[19] Robertson, *Grammar*, p. 113.

[20] The Greek text is capable of unambiguous meaning. It is true that sometimes it is ambiguous but in order to communicate multiple-points. The bottom line though, all

perceived ambiguity in the Greek New Testament is just that—*perceived*. We are the ones coming to the text with limited understanding of its meaning. We should never blame the text but recognize how languages works and realize that since we're not first century Greek speaking Christians there will be some things hard for us to understand. Still the perspicuity of the New Testament is intact for it is extremely clear on the essentials of the Christian faith (Galatians 1:8-9, Romans 8:1, Jude 3).

[21] A.T. Robertson is an important Greek expert for he wrote over 45 books and most on the Greek language. It's a mark of God's grace that on the day he died he had just finished teaching a class on the Greek language behind the Gospel of Matthew.

[22] J. Julius Scott Jr., *Customs and Controversies: Intertestamental Jewish Backgrounds of the New Testament* (Grand Rapids, Michigan: Baker Book House, 1995), p. 135.

[23] Ibid, 117.

[24] Machen, *Minister*.

[25] Ibid.

[26] I believe the Greek of the New Testament has a devotional and doxological component that is second to none. The Greek New Testament is a means of grace (it conveys God's love, peace and mercy) to the soul of the one who hears, sees and obeys its truths. I think this occurs in a measured process. In my experience, the process has five phases: education, enforcement, edification, enjoyment and exaltation. First, learning Greek simply educates your mind to the brilliance of the New Testament. Second, getting a taste of Greek allows you to see how vivid and clear it presents truth, which helps you to understand why Christian creeds were developed to enforce the truth of the unambiguous record of the Greek New Testament. Third, learning the nuances of the Greek New Testament builds up (edifies) your faith and confidence in God as well as your love for Him. Fourth, at some point the "charm of the Greek New Testament" simply enchants and attracts the reader to its treasure of delights, splendors and joys. Finally, the Greek words in the New Testament find their ultimate use in exalting the greatness, goodness and graciousness of the Lord. A Christian can truly say they know the "joy and power of the Greek New Testament" when they incorporate the Greek Scripture in their devotions, prayers and praises to God Most High.

[27] Font "TekniaGreek" used by permission, www.teknia.com.

[28] H.E. Dana and Julius R. Mantey, *A Manuel Grammar of the Greek New Testament* (New York: Macmillan Publishing Company, 1927), p. 266.

[29] *The Westminster Confession of Faith (*Signal Mountain, Tennessee: Summertown Texts, 1985 Revised EPC Edition), p. 5.

[30] Ibid., 27.

[31] Donald W. Burdick, *The Letters of John the Apostle* (Chicago: Moody Press, 1985), p. 402.

[32] Ibid., 218.

[33] Ibid, 219.

[34] John Calvin, *John* (Wheaton, Illinois: Crossway Books, 1994), p. 265.

[35] Burdick, 120-121.

[36] Daniel B. Wallace, *Greek Grammar Beyond The Basics* (Grand Rapids, Michigan: Zondervan Publishing House, 1996), p. 132.

[37] A. Berkeley Mickelsen, *Interpreting The Bible* (Grand Rapids, Michigan: Eerdmans Publishing Company, 1963), p. 14.

[38] *Chicago Statement of Inerrancy:* We affirm that the text of Scripture is to be interpreted by grammatico-historical exegesis, taking account of its literary forms and devices, and that Scripture is to interpret Scripture.

[39] Eugene Peterson, *Eat This Book* (C.S. Lewis Institute: Knowing and Doing Teaching Quarterly, 2003).

[40] *Westminster Confession of Faith:* The infallible rule of interpretation of Scripture is the Scripture itself: and therefore, when there is a question about the true and full sense of any Scripture (which is not manifold, but one), it must be searched and known by other places that speak more clearly.

[41] John H. Dobson, *Learn New Testament Greek* (Grand Rapids, Michigan: Baker Academic, 2005), pp. 282-283.

[42] Eugene Peterson says, "And it is disconcerting to find that a word that is used one way on page 26 is used in quite a different way on page 72 . . . Language is also constantly changing, in constant flux."

[43] R. C. Sproul, *Essential Truths Of The Christian Faith* (Wheaton, Illinois: Tyndale House Publishing, Inc, 1992), p. 115.

[44] In my previous book *Applying The Will Of God To The American Tragedy Of 9/11/01* (Publish America, 2004) I wrote: "So you may be asking, what should I be looking for as I read the Scriptures? Generally, God speaks to us in five distinct ways in the Holy Word (Psalm 119:50). First, God speaks to us through *mandates* that are clear and convicting commands that need to be obeyed (Psalm 119:59, 68, 71, 138). Second, He may communicate to us by drawing our attention to an inspiring Biblical character like King David who will act as a *model* from the pages of Scripture (Psalm 119:63, 75, 165). Third, God introduces us to a *mission* that He is directing us to participate in (Psalm 119:32, 133, 136). Fourth, God may provide us with an internal *motivation* that gives us strength to follow Him (Psalm 119:28, 107,127-128). Fifth, while we read the Scriptures we may become enthralled in the *majesty* of God's presence (Psalm 119:164-166). Gradually as we grow in the grace of God we become attuned to hearing our Creator's voice in all of these described ways (Psalm 119: 1-3, 9, 66, 97-105, 142, 144, 152-153)"

[45] These verses are taken from *The New American Standard Bible* (Chicago: Moody Press, 1975).

[46] My recommendation is Alfred Marshall's *The Interlinear NASB-NIV Parallel New Testament In Greek And English* (Grand Rapids, Michigan: Zondervan Publishing House, 1993). The Greek text used in this interlinear is the 21st edition of the Eberhard Nestle's *Novum Testamentum Graece*.

[47] *Chicago Statement of Inerrancy: Transmission and Translation*

Since God has nowhere promised an inerrant transmission of Scripture, it is necessary to affirm that only the autographic text of the original documents was inspired and to maintain the need of textual criticism as a means of detecting any slips that may have crept into the text in the course of its transmission. The verdict of this science, however, is that the Hebrew and Greek text appears to be amazingly well preserved, so that we are amply justified in affirming, with the Westminster Confession, a singular providence of God in this matter and in declaring that the authority of Scripture is in no way jeopardized by the fact that the copies we possess are not entirely error-free.

Similarly, no translation is or can be perfect, and all translations are an additional step away from the autograph. Yet the verdict of linguistic science is that English-speaking Christians, at least, are exceedingly well served in these days with a host of excellent translations and have no cause for hesitating to conclude that the true Word of God is within their reach. Indeed, in view of the frequent repetition in Scripture of the main matters with which it deals and also of the Holy Spirit's constant witness to and through the Word, no serious translation of Holy Scripture will so destroy its meaning as to render it unable to make its reader "wise for salvation through faith in Christ Jesus" (2 Tim. 3:15).

[48] William L. Lane, H*ebrews 9-13* (WBC; Dallas, Texas: Word Books, 1991), pp. 529, 541.

[49] The nasty battle Christians wage over what is the best Bible translation is sad evidence that we are not conducing ourselves in a manner worthy of the Gospel of Christ (Philippians 1:27). The Apostle Paul said it best (Philippians 1:18) with" But what does matter? The important thing is that in every way, whether from false motives or true, Christ is preached. And because of this I rejoice." Our attitude should be one of rejoicing over that fact that there are so many descent translations of the New Testament available for people to read. For example, the Apostle Paul defines the Gospel in 1 Corinthians 15:1-8. This Gospel definition is faithfully recorded in the King James Version, the New American Standard Version and the New International Version. The veracity of the Gospel message is clearly conveyed to the reader in any of these three translations. Therefore, we should say, with Paul, "because of this *we* rejoice."

[50] John Owen once wrote, "And what perplexities, mistakes and errors, the ignorance of the *original languages* hath cast many expositors into . . . especially among those who pertinaciously adhere unto *one translation* . . . might be manifested by instances . . . without number."

[51] Making the correct application to your life in your bible study is equally important as making the right interpretation. The best application method is to follow the example of Ezra in the Old Testament. Ezra 7:10 says, "For Ezra had devoted himself to the study and observance of the Law of the Lord, and to teaching its decrees and laws in Israel." I call this the **S.O.S.** method of bible study and application. First, you must **study** the Word of God (Ezra devoted himself to study). Second, you must **obey** and put into practice what you read (Ezra devoted himself to . . . the observance of the Law). Third, in order to really know the bible you must **share** its treasures with others (Ezra devoted himself to . . . teaching its decrees). This Ezra bible study process is the best in terms of integrating the Word of God into your daily life. It is helpful to ask yourself the question, "Does this Bible verse contain a promise, command, warning, teaching, prayer or example for my life?"

[52] D. Edmond Hiebert, *Titus and Philemon* (Chicago: Moody Press, 1957), p. 22.

[53] Charles C. Ryrie, What *You Should Know About Inerrancy* (Chicago: The Moody Bible Institute, 1981), pp. 38-41.

[54] *Chicago Statement of Inerrancy:* We affirm that Scripture in its entirety is inerrant, being free from all falsehood, fraud, or deceit.

[55] My philosophy of teaching Greek compels me to connect all my Greek grammar points to the New Testament text (Matthew 5:18, if not even an *Iota* will be lost in God's word, then we should let the New Testament itself teach us its Greek riches). This is why I call this course *Impact Greek* because I desire for the reader to immediately get a first hand

look at how Greek will *impact* their life for good. As A.T. Robertson said, ". . . the words of Jesus still fascinate the mind and win men to God as of old."

[56] J. Ramsey Michaels, *1 Peter* (WBC: Waco, Texas; Word Books, 1988), pp. 20-21.
[57] Ibid, 65-66.
[58] Mounce, *Basics of Biblical Greek*, p. 93.

Printed in Great Britain by
Amazon.co.uk, Ltd.,
Marston Gate.